ESSE

THE FOUR SEASONS COOKBOOK

First published in 2013 by Esse Engineering Limited,
Ouzledale Factory, Long Ing, Barnoldswick, Lancashire, BB18 6BN
www.esse.com

Cataloguing in Publication Data: a catalogue record for this book
is available from the British Library.

ISBN: 978-0-9576716-0-7

Designed by Andrea Rumsey, Rumseyshort
www.rumseyshort.co.uk
Printed by Aaron Printing Ltd

CONTENTS

FOREWORD

I have been cooking on range-style cookers
for over 30 years and on Esse ones for over 15!
Since I discovered them they have been my
range cooker of choice.

ONLINE RECIPE RESOURCE

With the help of River Cottage,
we're building an online recipe
resource for Esse owners.

As with this book, there is
an emphasis on regional
ingredients and seasonality,
so that you can get the best
from your range cooker and
enjoy the best of British food
in the process.

You can find these recipes in
the Esse TV section of the
website.

www.esse.com

During that time I have tested many variations from gas,
wood-fuelled and electric to the latest induction. All have their
merits and devotees.

One thing rings true… Esse nods to tradition when it comes to
their cookers and heritage but not at the expense of innovation…
they constantly look at new developments and trends in cooker
design for modern day cooking and living.

This cookery book, an Esse original first, celebrates what I believe as
a food writer matters and what Esse as a company engages with. We
both believe that good food comes from locally-sourced and ethically-
produced supplies and we recognise the need to follow the seasons.
By doing so we are generally eating food in its prime, at its most
economical and most readily available near to our doorsteps. Nature
will ensure the virtues of variety in the diet with such an approach.

On the following pages you will see how this approach is put into
practice when we follow the seasons through recipes for special
calendar dates.

So whether you are thinking ahead to Christmas and want a
fool-proof roast turkey or ham idea; looking for a 'flipping' good
pancake recipe for Shrove Tuesday; searching for family food for
Hallowe'en or Bonfire Night; or simply planning a picnic where you
can slip off your shoes and relax on a rug with some fine alfresco
fare… then you'll find some ideas to suit here.

Carol Bowen Ball

GREAT BRITISH BAKEWARE & ACCESSORIES FROM ESSE

I confess to having a whole arsenal of cookware handed down through the generations in my kitchen cupboards. Why? Well because good cooking utensils and bakeware lasts and sometimes improves with age. If something is used on a regular basis it means it has beneficial qualities.

I was always perplexed as to why Esse didn't have their own range and asked the question... thankfully now they do and it's a fine British range.

This new oven-safe range of hard anodised, heavy-duty black, two-toned enamelled and silver bakeware will help you cook perfect savoury, sweet and speciality cooked dishes, time after time. It's been designed for easy storage, easy cleaning and an aid to getting the perfect results.

I have put it through its paces as indeed has Gill Meller, River Cottage Head Chef, and we both use and like it.

So whether you're baking bread, cooking a quiche or preparing a lasagne for a from-the-dish eating experience, you'll find it in the Esse range.

BEFORE YOU BEGIN

It is important to remember that not only do different models of Esse cookers differ in their cooking action but, because they are hand-built, there can also be a little variation from one cooker to another within the same range. You will need to factor in a little 'getting-to-know-you' time when first installed.

The good news is that the indirect heat of an Esse is very forgiving which means it is not usually essential to cook at the exact temperature required in a recipe. Sometimes it may just be a matter of shelf position to achieve the right temperature rather than homing in on the exact dial reading. Your Owner's Companion will point you in the right direction to begin with and experience over time will pay huge rewards and dividends.

That said, the recipes in this book have been tested several times for accuracy, and the temperatures and times stated for cooking will ensure success. You are urged however to err on the side of safety by checking at the minimum time given.

Recognising that you may also want to convert some family favourite recipes, here is a guide to temperature conversions when cooking in the Esse.

OVEN TEMPERATURE EQUIVALENTS

100-120°C/Fan 80-100°C/Esse Dial Guide COOL. (Aim for the dial reading to be at the low end of COOL).

130°C/Fan 110°C/Esse Dial Guide COOL. (Aim for the dial to be in the middle of COOL).

140°C/Fan 120°C/Esse Dial Guide COOL. (Aim for the dial reading to be at the middle of COOL).

160°C/Fan 140°C/Esse Dial Guide MODERATE. (Aim for the dial reading to be at the low to middle end of MODERATE).

170°C/Fan 150°C/Esse Dial Guide MODERATE. (Aim for the dial reading to be in the middle of MODERATE).

180°C/Fan 160°C/Esse Dial Guide MODERATE. (Aim for the dial reading to be at the top end of MODERATE or very low end of HOT).

190°C/Fan 170°C/Esse Dial Guide HOT. (Aim for the dial reading to be at the low end of HOT).

200°C/Fan 180°C/Esse Dial Guide HOT. (Aim for the dial reading to be in the middle of HOT).

220°C/Fan 200°C/Esse Dial Guide HOT. (Aim for the dial reading to be at the top end of HOT).

230-240°C/Fan 210-220°C/Esse Dial Guide VERY HOT. (Aim for the dial reading to be at the low end of VERY HOT).

260°C/Fan 240°C/Esse Dial Guide VERY HOT. (Aim for the dial reading to be in the middle to top end of VERY HOT).

MEASUREMENTS AROUND THE WORLD

The measurements in the recipes in this book refer to metric quantities. If you wish to convert to US, Canadian or Australian cup and spoon measures or Imperial quantities then it is advisable to check and convert by using an online convertor programme or website.

REMEMBER...

- All spoon quantities are measured level unless otherwise stated.
- Eggs are large.
- Flour is plain; water is cold; and sugar is granulated unless stated differently.

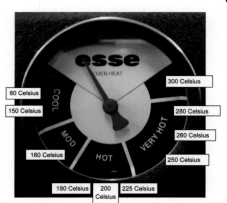

SPRING

Spring heralds its arrival with the emergence of tender young vegetable shoots; early season, succulent lamb; and the very first cropping of Jersey Royal potatoes... all the better for serving with lush-leaved herbs.

All make welcome dishes to cook for those Spring treat days at Easter, for Mothering Sunday and Shrove Tuesday. It's the time to really shrug off Winter... and use up the stock of economical root or main crop vegetables in baked treats and light and airy pancakes... some might even become favourite seasonal newcomers to the table.

EASTER

GOOD FRIDAY

Warm Jersey Royal Salad with Seared Mackerel with mixed baby leaf salad

THE MAIN EVENT

Roasted British Asparagus with Chilli and Lime Butter

St Clement's Roast Lamb with roasted white and sweet potatoes, fennel, flageolet beans and redcurrant jelly

SWEET TREATS

Oaty Baked Strawberry Cheesecake

Easter Bunny Biscuits

MOTHERING SUNDAY

Big Breakfast Frittata with Smoky Beans

Parma Ham Pitta Pizzas

Beetroot and Vanilla Cupcakes

SHROVE TUESDAY

Wild Alaska Pollock and Prawn Pancakes *or*

Pink Lady French Crêpes

WARM JERSEY ROYAL SALAD WITH SEARED MACKEREL

Here is a fish dish that is perfect for Good Friday eating or great for a simple mid-week supper. Jersey Royal potatoes are simply unbeatable when available in the Spring but any other waxy potato can be used when out of season. A mixed baby leaf salad makes a fine accompaniment.

SERVES 4

450g Jersey Royal potatoes, scrubbed

2 spring onions, finely chopped

2 tbsp snipped chives

3 tbsp mayonnaise

salt and freshly ground black pepper

olive oil

4 fillets fresh mackerel

lemon wedges, to serve

1. Place the Jersey Royals in a pan of salted water, bring to the boil and simmer until the potatoes are cooked, about 15-25 minutes (depending upon size). Drain and cut any large potatoes into bite-sized pieces.

2. Add the spring onions, chives, mayonnaise and salt and pepper to taste and gently fold together. Keep warm while cooking the mackerel.

3. Lightly smear a frying pan with olive oil and heat until hot. Add the mackerel fillets, skin-side down, reduce the heat to a gentle sizzle and cook until golden brown, about 4-5 minutes. Flip over, season to taste and cook for a further minute or until the fish is cooked. Remove from the heat and allow to rest for 2 minutes.

4. To serve, place a portion of the warmed potato salad in the centre of 4 plates. Top each with a mackerel fillet. Serve at once with wedges of lemon to squeeze over the fish.

TIP

This dish needs nothing more than a simple baby leaf salad accompaniment. Consider leaves of watercress, corn salad, rocket, chard or spinach tossed in a citrusy lemon dressing.

ROASTED BRITISH ASPARAGUS WITH CHILLI AND LIME BUTTER

Roasting asparagus, instead of boiling or steaming, produces a starter or vegetable dish with a good intense flavour. Here it is served with a butter that has a zesty kick. It would make a wonderful light Spring lunch dish or a superb accompaniment for simple poached or baked salmon.

SERVES 4

100g butter

1 red chilli, deseeded and finely chopped

2 tbsp chopped fresh coriander

½ tsp cumin seeds, roughly ground

juice of ½ lime

salt and freshly ground black pepper

2 bundles British asparagus

olive oil

1 lime, cut into wedges

1. Preheat the oven if necessary to 200°C/Fan 180°C/Esse Dial Guide HOT. (Aim for the dial reading to be in the middle of HOT).

2. Bring the butter to room temperature then mix in the chilli, coriander, cumin, lime juice and salt and pepper to taste. Place on a sheet of cling film, roll into a sausage shape then chill until firm.

3. Trim the ends of the asparagus and place on a roasting tray. Drizzle with olive oil and season to taste with salt and freshly ground black pepper. Roast in the oven for 6-8 minutes until just tender but still with a little bite.

4. Transfer to 4 warmed serving plates. Top each with a slice of the prepared butter and a wedge of lime. Serve at once.

GET AHEAD!

The butter can be made up to 5 days ahead and stored in the refrigerator, ready for slicing when required. It is also delicious to serve with simply cooked fish fillets and chicken breasts.

ST CLEMENT'S ROAST LAMB

Easter wouldn't be Easter without this British classic. I've tweaked it a bit with the addition of orange and lemon... it rings the changes if you'll excuse the pun! I still like to serve it with my signature-dish of flageolet beans (with the lamb juices stirred in) but fennel is a great accompaniment too.

SERVES 6

2kg leg of lamb

2 oranges

salt and freshly ground black pepper

4 tbsp chopped fresh thyme leaves

2 lemons, sliced

3 tbsp dry white wine or white grape juice

1. Preheat the oven if necessary to 200°C/Fan 180°C/Esse Dial Guide HOT. (Aim for the dial reading to be in the middle of HOT).

2. Grate the zest from the oranges then cut the orange flesh into slices. Make several deep incisions over the surface of the lamb and season. Press the thyme and orange zest over the lamb and into the slits.

3. Place the orange and lemon slices in a large non-stick roasting tin and put the leg of lamb on the top. Open roast for about 1¼ hours for pink meat and about 1½ hours for medium to well-done meat, basting occasionally. About 30 minutes before the end of the cooking time pour the wine or grape juice over the lamb and continue to roast.

4. When cooked, cover with foil and leave to rest for 15 minutes before carving. Remove any excess fat from the cooking juices and use to make a gravy or jus if liked or stir into cooked seasonal vegetables or canned beans (like flageolet) as liked.

TIP

Roast potatoes or potatoes boulangère makes a fine accompaniment. Why not try roasting a mixture of white and sweet potatoes for variety?

OATY BAKED STRAWBERRY CHEESECAKE

This cheesecake looks stunning and tastes divine, yet takes only minutes to prepare. It can be topped with almost any prepared fruit of your choice and is wonderful with a little single cream to serve. If liked some sultanas or chopped stem ginger could be added to the basic cream cheese mixture.

SERVES 8

50g butter

50g clear honey

150g rolled porridge oats

400g cream cheese

3 medium eggs, separated

75g caster sugar

1 tsp vanilla essence

150g fresh strawberries, thinly sliced

mint sprigs, to garnish

1. Preheat the oven if necessary to 180°C/Fan 160°C/Esse Dial Guide MODERATE. (Aim for the dial reading to be at the top end of MODERATE or very low end of HOT).

2. Melt the butter and the honey in a pan then stir in the oats, mixing well. Press onto the base of a 20cm round, loose-bottomed cake tin.

3. Whisk the cream cheese with the egg yolks, sugar and vanilla essence until smooth.

4. Whisk the egg whites until stiff then fold into the cream cheese mixture. Pour into the cake tin.

5. Bake in the oven for 35-40 minutes or until golden and just firm to the touch. Allow to cool before removing from the tin and transferring to a serving plate.

6. Chill well then top with the sliced strawberries and mint to serve.

VARIATION

Oaty Baked Rhubarb Cheesecake: Prepare as above but top with 225g cooked rhubarb mixed with 5 tbsp warmed preserve. Rhubarb compôte is particularly good.

EASTER BUNNY BISCUITS

Children will enjoy making these buttery biscuits with currants and spice for family and friends over the Easter holidays. They are also perfect to wrap for Easter gifts... often a welcome change from the chocolate eggstravaganza!

MAKES 20-25

125g softened butter

75g caster sugar, plus 1-2 tbsp extra for sprinkling

1 egg, separated

200g plain flour

½ tsp ground cinnamon

½ tsp ground mixed spice

grated zest of 1 lemon

75g currants

2 tbsp milk

1. Preheat the oven to 200°C/Fan 180°C/Esse Dial Guide HOT. (Aim for the dial reading to be in the middle of HOT).

2. Beat the butter with the sugar until pale and fluffy. Beat in the egg yolk then gently stir in the flour, cinnamon, mixed spice, lemon zest and currants. Gradually stir in the milk until the dough starts to come together... you may need slightly less or more of the milk.

3. Turn out onto a lightly floured surface and knead until smooth. Roll out until about 5mm thick then stamp out the biscuits using a round 7.5cm cutter or shape of your choice.

4. Place on 2-3 greased baking trays and cook in the oven for 10 minutes. Remove from the oven. Whisk the egg white just a little to break up, brush lightly over the biscuits and sprinkle with the caster sugar. Return to the oven for a further 5 minutes until just golden. Remove and cool on a wire rack.

5. Store in an airtight tin for 2-3 days.

GET AHEAD!

The biscuits can be made ahead and stored in an airtight tin for 2-3 days. Freshen by placing them in a warm oven for 3-4 minutes.

BIG BREAKFAST FRITTATA WITH SMOKY BEANS

Mother's Day for many means the treat of 'breakfast in bed'. This recipe hits the spot every time for me... it's a variation of a 'Full English' with eggs, sausage, bacon, potatoes and tomatoes in one pan with a side portion of smoky beans. It's simple enough for any teenager to prepare and it can also be made well ahead and just reheated (by those who dislike early mornings).

SERVES 4

sunflower or olive oil

1 onion, cut into 6 wedges

225g new potatoes, cooked and sliced

2 sausages, cooked and sliced

2 rashers lean back bacon, cooked and chopped

5 eggs

salt and freshly ground black pepper

2 tbsp chopped fresh parsley

6 cherry tomatoes, halved (optional)

400g can baked beans

½-1 tsp smoked paprika

1. Smear a large non-stick frying pan (with heatproof handle) liberally with sunflower or olive oil. Heat, add the onion and cook for about 6-7 minutes or until browned.

2. Add the potatoes, sausage and bacon. Cook for a further 7 minutes, shaking the pan occasionally.

3. Beat the eggs with seasoning to taste and the parsley. Pour gently over the potato mixture to cover evenly. Return to a low heat and cook gently for a further 15 minutes until the eggs are just set. Add the tomatoes to the top if using.

4. Meanwhile, preheat the grill until hot. Place the frittata under the grill and cook for 2-3 minutes until the top is lightly browned. Alternatively place in a very hot oven and cook until the top is lightly browned.

5. At the same time, place the beans in a pan with the smoked paprika and heat until hot. Serve the frittata cut into wedges with a portion of beans on the side.

GET AHEAD!

The frittata can be prepared a day ahead then chilled until required. Reheat in a moderate oven until hot, about 10-15 minutes. The smoky beans are best made fresh.

PARMA HAM PITTA PIZZAS

Some mothers are taken out for a meal on Mothering Sunday and some enjoy a meal prepared for them at home. My own children came up with this real winner a couple of years ago... a pizza made with a ready-made base but imaginative topping that can be on the table in next to no time. They used naan bread instead of pitta for theirs but both work fabulously well.

SERVES 4

8 tsp regular or sun-dried tomato purée

8 mini or 4 large white or wholemeal pitta breads

4 medium tomatoes, sliced

2 tsp dried Italian mixed herbs

100g mozzarella cheese, grated

freshly ground black pepper

8 black or green olives

8 slices Parma ham

basil leaves, to garnish

1. Preheat the grill to medium/hot or the oven if necessary to 190˚C/Fan 170˚C/Esse Dial Guide HOT. (Aim for the dial reading to be at the low end of HOT).

2. Divide and spread the tomato purée evenly over one side of each pitta bread. Arrange on the grill rack or on a baking tray and top with the sliced tomatoes. Sprinkle with the mixed herbs, grated mozzarella and pepper to taste.

3. Grill for 3-4 minutes or bake in the oven for 6-8 minutes until the cheese is melted and bubbling. Top with the olives and Parma ham. Scatter over a few basil leaves and serve at once.

VARIATION

Parma Ham and Pesto Pitta Pizzas: Prepare as above but replace the tomato purée with red or green pesto and omit the dried Italian mixed herbs.

BEETROOT AND VANILLA CUPCAKES

These dainty little cupcakes with their rose butter icing will make the perfect Mother's Day gift. Top each with a ready-made flower decoration or crystallised rose petal. To make your own see GET AHEAD! below.

MAKES 12

175g unsalted butter

175g caster sugar

3 large eggs, separated

175g self-raising flour

175g plain cooked beetroot, puréed (with a little juice reserved for the icing)

1 tbsp vanilla essence

Icing:

300g icing sugar

150g unsalted butter

few drops rose flower water

12 ready-made flower decorations or crystallised rose petals, to decorate

1. Preheat the oven if necessary to 180°C/Fan 160°C/Esse Dial Guide MODERATE. (Aim for the dial reading to be at the top end of MODERATE or very low end of HOT). Line a 12-hole cupcake tray with cases.

2. Cream the butter with the sugar until light and fluffy. Add the egg yolks, flour, puréed beetroot and vanilla and beat until smooth.

3. In a clean bowl whisk the egg whites until fairly stiff. Take a large spoon of the egg white and beat into the flour mixture to loosen a little, then gently fold the remaining egg white through the mixture.

4. Divide between the cupcake cases and bake for 20 minutes, or until the cakes are firm to the touch. Remove to cool on a rack.

5. Meanwhile, to make the icing, beat the icing sugar with the butter until fluffy. Add a few drops of rose flower water and a few drops of the reserved beetroot juice to flavour and lightly colour, mixing well. Spread generously or pipe over the cooled cupcakes and decorate with a flower or petal to serve.

GET AHEAD!

To make your own crystallised rose petals then prepare at least the day before they are required. They will keep in an airtight box for a few weeks. Lay out a piece of silicone-coated baking paper on a tray. Brush 12 organic rose petals with egg white and sprinkle all over with caster sugar. Allow to dry in a warm place for 8 hours before using.

WILD ALASKA POLLOCK AND PRAWN PANCAKES

This Shrove Tuesday, why not add a twist to your normal pancake repertoire, by making these scrumptious savoury pancakes? They're made by simply adding flakes of pollock and prawns to a creamy cheese and herb sauce that's perfect for filling home-made pancakes.

GET AHEAD!

The pancakes can be made ahead and placed in a large greased baking dish. Cover with foil and chill. Reheat in the oven at 180°C/Fan 160°C/Esse Dial Guide MODERATE. (Aim for the dial reading to be at the top end of MODERATE or very low end of HOT) for about 10 minutes.

SERVES 4

400g smoked wild Alaska pollock

Pancakes:

100g plain flour

salt and freshly ground black pepper

1 medium egg

300ml milk

vegetable oil for cooking

Sauce:

300ml milk

40g butter

40g plain flour

100g mature Cheddar cheese, grated

75g cooked peeled prawns

1 tbsp chopped fresh parsley, dill or chives

1. Put the smoked pollock in a frying pan and cover with water. Heat and simmer for 5-6 minutes until the fish is cooked. The flesh should be opaque and should flake easily. Drain and cool, then flake into large chunks. Set aside.

2. To make the pancakes, put the flour, a little seasoning and egg in a bowl. Gradually whisk in the milk to make a smooth batter.

3. Heat a medium heavy-based frying pan and add a few drops of oil. Pour in a ladleful of the batter, swirl the pan to make a thin pancake and cook for 1-2 minutes, turning halfway through until golden and cooked. Transfer to a warmed plate and repeat to make a total of 8 pancakes.

4. To make the sauce, put the milk, butter and flour in a pan. Heat, whisking constantly, until smooth and thickened. Add the cheese and stir to melt. Add the pollock, prawns, seasoning to taste and most of the herbs. Heat gently then use to fill the pancakes. Sprinkle with the remaining herbs to serve.

PINK LADY FRENCH CRÊPES

This recipe is loosely based on the classic French crêpe suzette but uses sweet apples as well as orange and lemon. It would be lovely served with a scoop of vanilla ice cream on Shrove Tuesday.

SERVES 4

Crêpes:

125g plain flour

1 vanilla pod, split in half

2 large eggs

200ml milk

15g butter, melted plus extra for cooking

Topping:

150ml fresh orange juice

grated zest of 1 orange and 1 lemon

3 tbsp caster sugar

3 cardamom pods, crushed

30g butter, melted

2 Pink Lady apples, cored, thickly sliced and slices halved

1. To make the crêpes, put the flour and vanilla seeds in a bowl and add the eggs. Gradually whisk in the milk and butter to make a smooth batter.

2. Heat a large frying pan and brush with a little extra melted butter. Pour in a ladleful of the batter, swirl the pan to make a large thin pancake and cook for 1-2 minutes, turning halfway through until golden and cooked. Fold into quarters, transfer to a warm plate and keep warm. Repeat with the remaining batter to make 4 large crêpes in total.

3. To make the topping, put the orange juice, orange and lemon zest, sugar and cardamom pods into the frying pan and bring to the boil. Gradually stir in the melted butter. Add the apples and crêpes and gently warm through, tossing in the sauce. Serve at once.

TIP

Adults might like the addition of 2 tbsp Curaçao or Grand Marnier to the topping for a special occasion.

SUMM🦋R

Baskets, generously packed with picnic fare or piled high with soft fruits (picked fresh from the stem), reflect that Summer is really here. Summer eating is all about indulging in the pleasant delights of such abundant crops of vegetables and fruit but also provides the best excuse to shake out the rug or dust off the hamper for some irresistibly festive eating out of doors.

It's also the time to celebrate some mainly manly dishes for Father's Day and sturdy dishes for man-sized appetites at the start of the game season on The Glorious 12th.

FATHER'S DAY

Quick Shepherd's Pie for a Special Pa

Viva Strawberry and Macadamia Blondies

A POSH PICNIC

THE MAIN EVENT

Cheesy Picnic Bread with Pepperoni and Tomatoes with dips like hummous and guacamole *or*

Shallot Dartois with cherry tomatoes, salad and fresh fruit *or*

Green Pesto Turkey Salad and crusty bread *or*

Spiced Chicken with Mango Salsa with couscous

SWEET TREAT

Sweet Eve Strawberry and Lavender Eton Mess

THE GLORIOUS 12TH

Ginger and Carrot Soup with Lemon Herb Cream with crusty wholemeal bread

Pot Roast Pheasant with Fenland Celery with mashed potato, buttered greens or broccoli

Summer Berry and Lemon Curd Cream Pavlova

QUICK SHEPHERD'S PIE FOR A SPECIAL PA

I don't know a man who doesn't appreciate a home-cooked comforting nursery food dish on Father's Day... other than perhaps opting for a steak fest! But nursery classics can be time and energy intensive and baffle or preclude some of the younger members of the family. This was my own children's answer to the dilemma – a classic type Shepherd's Pie but with a quick and easy topping. I make no excuses for the use of gravy granules in this dish... it means it's fool-proof. The garlic bread 'crown' also means the dish can be on the table in just 30 minutes!

SERVES 4

500g lamb mince

1 onion, finely chopped

2 carrots, peeled and chopped

1 tsp dried rosemary

2 tbsp onion gravy granules

2 tbsp Worcestershire sauce

100g frozen peas

2 frozen garlic baguettes

1 tbsp olive oil

1. Preheat the oven if necessary to 200°C/Fan 180°C/Esse Dial Guide HOT. (Aim for the dial reading to be in the middle of HOT).

2. In a large pan, fry the lamb mince with the onion, carrots and rosemary for 5 minutes, stirring frequently.

3. Add the gravy granules, Worcestershire sauce, peas and 100ml boiling water, mixing well. Cover and simmer for 10 minutes, stirring occasionally, then transfer to an ovenproof dish.

4. Slice the garlic bread and arrange over the top of the lamb mixture. Drizzle the bread with the olive oil and bake for 15 minutes until golden. Serve, if liked, with a crisp green salad.

> **TIP**
>
> The garlic baguettes can be replaced with a ready-made tear-and-share bread offering. The cheese, onion and garlic variety is a good Father pleasing option.

VIVA STRAWBERRY AND MACADAMIA BLONDIES

What Dad doesn't like a sweet treat on Father's Day? These are a great alternative to the traditional chocolate brownie, bursting with strawberries, white chocolate and nuts. Perfect as an afternoon or morning coffee treat, they are equally delicious as a pudding.

MAKES 16

125g unsalted butter

200g white chocolate

2 eggs

100g light muscovado sugar

130g plain flour

pinch of salt

120g Viva strawberries, chopped

100g macadamia nuts, roughly chopped

1. Preheat the oven if necessary to 180°C/Fan 160°C/Esse Dial Guide MODERATE. (Aim for the dial reading to be at the top end of MODERATE or very low end of HOT).

2. Line a 22cm square baking tin with greaseproof paper.

3. Place the butter in a pan, heat to melt then cook on a low heat for 5 minutes or until the white solids start to turn golden. Pour into a cold bowl, add half of the chocolate and stir until melted.

4. In a separate bowl, whisk the eggs with the sugar until they are thick and golden. Add the flour, salt, prepared chocolate butter and fold in with a spatula until smooth.

5. Add the strawberries, nuts and remaining chocolate and stir briefly to combine. Pour into the prepared dish or tin and bake for 30 minutes. The Blondies are cooked when they have a light golden crust but are still a little squidgy inside. Allow to cool in the dish or tin then cut into 16 pieces to serve.

GET AHEAD!

The Blondies can be made ahead and will keep for 1-2 days if stored in an airtight tin – if they last that long!

CHEESY PICNIC BREAD WITH PEPPERONI AND TOMATOES

This moreish picnic bread is great served warm with dips like hummous or guacamole. Keep warm wrapped in foil and a tea towel for transporting. If you don't want to make the bread from scratch, use a bread mix (see GET AHEAD!).

MAKES 12 SLICES

Bread:

300ml tepid water

1 tbsp dried yeast

500g strong plain bread flour

1 tsp salt

2 tbsp finely chopped sun-dried tomatoes in oil

2 tbsp grated Parmesan cheese

OR 500g pack bread mix
(I used Wright's Parmesan and Sun Dried Tomato Mix)

Filling:

125g mozzarella, roughly torn

70g sliced pepperoni

100g baby plum tomatoes, halved and deseeded

15g fresh basil leaves, roughly torn

1. Preheat the oven if necessary to 220°C/Fan 200°C/Esse Dial Guide HOT) (Aim for the dial reading to be at the top end of HOT).

2. Place half the water in a bowl, sprinkle over the yeast and leave to stand for 15 minutes.

3. Mix the flour with the salt, yeast mixture, tomatoes, Parmesan and remaining water and mix to a soft dough. Knead for 5 minutes, cover and prove in a warm place until doubled in size, about 1 hour.

4. Turn onto a lightly floured surface and knead for 2 minutes. Roll out to a 30 x 40cm oblong then cut in half lengthways. Scatter the mozzarella pieces, pepperoni, tomatoes and basil over both halves. Working from the longest side, tightly roll up each piece of dough. Place on lightly greased baking trays, cover with cling film and leave in a warm place for 40 minutes until doubled in size.

5. Bake for 30-35 minutes until well-risen, golden and cooked. Allow to cool slightly before slicing to serve.

GET AHEAD!

The picnic bread can be made with a bread mix. Make up according to the pack instructions and knead until smooth. Leave to rest for 5 minutes. Roll out, prove and bake as above.

SHALLOT DARTOIS

This is the vegetarian equivalent of the traditional sausage roll... where the usual sausage meat has been replaced with a deeply-satisfying shallot mixture. Meat lovers could add a little very finely chopped ham or chicken to the shallot mixture.

SERVES 4

100g butter

24 echalion (banana) shallots, peeled and finely sliced lengthways

salt and freshly ground black pepper

1 bottle red wine

10g chopped fresh thyme

50g caster sugar

320g pack pre-rolled puff pastry

beaten egg, to glaze

1. Preheat the oven if necessary to 200°C/Fan 180°C/Esse Dial Guide HOT. (Aim for the dial reading to be in the middle of HOT).

2. Melt the butter in a heavy-based pan until sizzling. Add the shallots with seasoning to taste and cook for about 10 minutes.

3. Add the wine, thyme and sugar and continue to cook until all the liquid has evaporated. You should be left with a rich, deep, dark red shallot mixture. Allow to cool.

4. Cut the sheet of pastry lengthways in half and, with a rolling pin, carefully roll to make each rectangle a little wider. Spoon half the filling along each in a sausage shape, leaving a small margin. Brush with egg and fold the pastry over to enclose the filling, pressing down firmly. Brush with egg and chill for 30 minutes.

5. To cook, cut each dartois into 5cm slices and place on a non-stick baking tray or conventional one lined with easy glide. Bake for 12-15 minutes until golden. Serve warm or cold.

GET AHEAD!

The shallot mixture can be made up to 2 days in advance. Chill until required.

GREEN PESTO TURKEY SALAD

This salad looks and tastes stunning, yet takes no time to prepare at all. When the sun decides to shine this is perfect for an informal picnic lunch with friends and family.

SERVES 4

600ml chicken stock

400g fresh turkey breast strips

100g roasted red peppers (from a jar), sliced

1 small iceberg lettuce, roughly chopped

10 cherry tomatoes, halved

25g toasted pine nuts

Dressing:

150ml mayonnaise

3 tbsp ready-made green pesto

2 tsp snipped chives

2 tsp chopped fresh parsley

4 spring onions, chopped

15g grated Parmesan cheese

3 tbsp white wine vinegar

2 tbsp cold water

salt and freshly ground black pepper

1. Bring the stock to a boil in a pan. Add the turkey strips and simmer for 8-10 minutes, or until thoroughly cooked. Drain, allow to cool and cut any large strips into bite-sized pieces.

2. Toss the cooled turkey with the peppers, lettuce, tomatoes and pine nuts in a serving bowl or transportable dish.

3. Meanwhile, to make the dressing, place the mayonnaise in a jug with the pesto, chives, parsley, spring onions and half of the Parmesan. Whisk in the vinegar and water to make a loose dressing. Season to taste with salt and freshly ground black pepper.

4. Drizzle the turkey mixture with the dressing and sprinkle with the remaining cheese to serve. This is delicious served with crusty bread.

VARIATION

Coronation Turkey Salad:
Prepare the turkey as above but mix with a light curried dressing. Prepare by mixing 75ml mayonnaise with 75ml natural yogurt, 2 tsp curry paste, grated zest and juice of 1 orange, 1 tsp grated root ginger, 1 tsp chopped red chilli and salt and pepper to taste.

SPICED CHICKEN WITH MANGO SALSA

This zingy spiced chicken with fruity but cooling salsa is delicious both hot and cold. I like to serve it cold as a picnic dish with a rocket leaf salad and plain or herby couscous. Toss the salad in a lemon or lime-based dressing for a memorable meal.

SERVES 6

juice of 1 lemon

2 tbsp olive oil

1½ tbsp Jerk seasoning

12 chicken thigh fillets

Salsa:

2 ripe mangoes, peeled and chopped

200g natural yogurt

1 red onion, very finely chopped

10g chopped fresh coriander

1. Place the lemon juice, oil and Jerk seasoning in a large bowl. Add the chicken fillets and stir to coat. Cover and chill for at least 1 hour or ideally overnight to allow the flavours to develop.

2. When ready to cook preheat the oven if necessary to 200°C/Fan 180°C/Esse Dial Guide HOT). (Aim for the dial reading to be in the middle of HOT).

3. Place the chicken on a rack over a roasting tin and cook in the oven for 30 minutes, until tender and cooked through. To check, pierce the chicken flesh, the juices should run clear.

4. Meanwhile, make the salsa by mixing the mango with the yogurt, red onion and coriander.

5. Serve the chicken hot or cold with the mango salsa.

VARIATION

The spicy chicken can be served with an avocado salsa instead. Simply mix the flesh of 1 ripe chopped avocado with half a small chopped red onion, 2 chopped tomatoes, the juice of half a lime and salt and pepper to taste. Serve sprinkled with chopped coriander if liked.

SWEET EVE STRAWBERRY AND LAVENDER ETON MESS

Meringues made in the Esse are quite magical but are best made when the oven temperature is low so that they do not cook and brown beyond a pale blonde colour. Thankfully they can be made when the oven temperature is COOL then stored in an airtight tin until required. Here they are mixed with berries, cream and lavender for a take on Eton Mess.

SERVES 4

3 egg whites

175g caster sugar

500ml double cream

2 tbsp icing sugar

4 lavender flower heads, finely chopped and a few extra to decorate

400g Sweet Eve strawberries, hulled and chopped

1. Preheat the oven if necessary to 140°C/Fan 120°C/Esse Dial Guide COOL. (Aim for the dial reading to be in the middle of COOL). Or allow the oven temperature to drop to COOL.

2. Whisk the egg whites until soft peaks form. Add the caster sugar, a spoonful at a time, whisking well until stiff and glossy. Pipe or spoon onto a baking tray lined with silicone paper. Bake for about 1-1½ hours until firm and dry. Allow to cool.

3. Whip the cream until just stiff and fold in the icing sugar and chopped lavender.

4. Place half of the strawberries in a blender and purée. Add to the cream mixture with the remaining strawberries and coarsely broken up meringues, mixing gently.

5. To serve, spoon into bowls or vintage teacups and top with extra lavender heads to decorate.

GET AHEAD!

You can make this pudding well ahead... it can be chilled in the refrigerator for several hours before serving and will also keep well in a coolie box (with ice pack) for transporting on a picnic.

GINGER AND CARROT SOUP WITH LEMON HERB CREAM

This colourful and vibrant ginger and carrot soup is deliciously smooth and comforting but does have a bit of a kick. Don't be tempted to omit the lemon herb cream topping... it lifts this soup into the luxury class. Serve with crusty wholemeal bread for a substantial starter or lunch dish. If freezing the soup do so without the topping.

SERVES 4

3 tbsp olive oil

600g carrots, peeled and chopped

2 onions, chopped

1 clove garlic, crushed

1 tsp ground ginger

1 tsp medium curry powder

1.5 litres good vegetable stock

pared rind of 1 lemon

salt and freshly ground black pepper

Lemon Herb Cream:

200g crème fraîche

finely grated rind of 1 lemon

2 tsp chopped fresh parsley

2 tsp snipped chives

1 carrot, peeled and grated, to garnish (optional)

1. Heat the olive oil in a large pan. Add the carrots and onions and cook gently for 5-8 minutes, stirring occasionally. Add the garlic, ginger and curry powder and cook for 1 minute.

2. Add the stock, lemon strips and salt and pepper to taste. Half cover the pan with its lid, and simmer gently for about 20 minutes or until the carrots are very tender.

3. Cool slightly then purée until smooth. Return the soup to the pan, taste and adjust the seasoning if necessary and reheat to serve.

4. To make the topping, mix the crème fraîche with the lemon rind, parsley and chives.

5. To serve, ladle the soup into warmed bowls and top each with a spoonful of the prepared lemon herb cream. Garnish with a little grated carrot if liked.

TIP

If preferred top the soup with fried bread croûtons but toss them in grated Parmesan cheese or chopped herbs after cooking for a crunchy topping with attitude!

POT ROAST PHEASANT WITH FENLAND CELERY

Pot roasting pheasant produces a beautifully tender bird where the meat literally falls from the bone. Serve with creamy mashed potato and some buttered greens or broccoli for a deeply satisfying meal.

SERVES 4-6

50g butter

2 tbsp olive oil

2 oven-ready pheasants

6 shallots, peeled and cut in half

4 large sticks Fenland celery, each cut into 3 pieces

3 cloves garlic, sliced

2 tsp fennel seeds, lightly crushed

salt and freshly ground black pepper

500ml white wine

1. Preheat the oven if necessary to 160°C/Fan 140°C/Esse Dial Guide MODERATE. (Aim for the dial reading to be at the low to middle end of MODERATE).

2. Melt the butter with the olive oil in a large flameproof casserole that is large enough to hold both pheasants snugly. When foaming, add a pheasant and fry until crisp and golden on all sides. Transfer to a plate and cook the second pheasant in the same way. Transfer to the plate.

3. Reduce the heat, add the shallots and cook for 10 minutes until softened. Add the celery, garlic, fennel seeds and salt and pepper to taste. Pour in the wine and return the pheasants to the dish. Bring to a simmer, then cover and cook in the oven for 1-1½ hours, until the meat is very tender.

4. Remove the pheasants from the dish and divide into serving pieces. Keep warm while simmering the sauce on the hob until slightly thickened. Serve with the meat.

TIP

For a glossier and slightly more thickened sauce stir 2 tbsp conserve into the juices after reducing. Blackcurrant or Wild Blueberry conserve are ideal choices.

SUMMER BERRY AND LEMON CURD CREAM PAVLOVA

I adore pavlova with its crisp shell yet softer, almost marshmallow-like centre and it's all the better when piled with Summer berries. Adding some lemon curd to the whipped cream topping gives it a zesty citrus flavour that is hard to beat.

SERVES 6-8

3 large egg whites

175g caster sugar

1 tsp cornflour

1 tsp vanilla essence

1 tsp white wine vinegar

300ml double cream

4 tbsp lemon curd

100g blueberries

150g strawberries, hulled and halved

1. Preheat the oven if necessary to 130°C/Fan 110°C/Esse Dial Guide COOL. (Aim for the dial reading to be in the middle of COOL).

2. Line a baking tray with baking parchment and draw a 23cm circle in the centre.

3. Whisk the egg whites until they form stiff peaks. Add half the caster sugar and whisk again until the mixture is thick and glossy. Mix the cornflour, vanilla and sugar to a paste and fold into the eggs with the remaining sugar.

4. Pile the meringue into the circle, making a hollow in the centre (to hold the cream and fruit topping). Bake for about 1½ hours or until a blonde colour, crispy on the outside but a little soft in the centre. Allow to cool.

5. To serve, whip the cream until it forms soft peaks. Fold in the lemon curd and pile on top of the meringue. Top with the blueberries and strawberries to serve.

GET AHEAD!

The filling can be added to the meringue up to 1 hour before serving.

AUTUMN

Autumn is the season of mellow fruitfulness, when the rich harvest of the Summer is complete and there is a treasury of fruit and vegetables for using in soups, bakes, roasts and sweet treats. Days are getting much shorter but there is welcoming flickering cheer in the form of Hallowe'en and Bonfire Night.

Wrap up warm and enjoy some consolatory heart and soul warming seasonal favourites from the selection here for your Harvest Festival or Guy Fawkes menus... they will delight young and old eaters alike.

HARVEST FESTIVAL

THE MAIN EVENT

Parmigiano-Reggiano and Butternut Squash Soup *or*

Wild Alaska Salmon Korma Bake *or*

Five Spiced Pork with Roots

SWEET TREATS

Saffron Poached Pears with Parmigiano-Reggiano

Lemon Tart with Fresh Fruit Topping

HALLOWE'EN

Penne with Roast Shallots and Pumpkin Seeds

Sticky Ginger and Beetroot Muffins

BONFIRE NIGHT

Roasted Tomato Soup with Crispy Bacon and crusty bread *or*

Mini Sausage Wraps with Crispy Onions *or*

Bonfire Pumpkin Pilaf with Almonds

PARMIGIANO-REGGIANO AND BUTTERNUT SQUASH SOUP

This superb soup has a fantastic taste, enhanced by adding the rind from the cheese as it cooks, to extract every bit of flavour. You'll need roughly 500g butternut squash when peeled and deseeded. If you have any leftover, simply roast to serve as a vegetable with another meal.

SERVES 4-6

150g Parmigiano-Reggiano cheese, with rind

25g butter

1 large onion, finely chopped

1 medium butternut squash, peeled, deseeded and chopped into chunks

900ml hot vegetable stock

150ml milk

salt and freshly ground black pepper

4-6 slices French bread

chopped fresh parsley or thyme, to garnish

1. Reserve the rind from the Parmigiano-Reggiano and cut into chunks, then finely grate the cheese.

2. Melt the butter in a large pan, add the onion and cook gently for about 3 minutes, until softened but not browned. Add the squash, stock and cheese rind. Heat until the mixture is just simmering, then partially cover with a lid and cook gently for about 20 minutes, until the vegetables are soft and tender.

3. Remove the rind from the pan and discard. Purée the mixture with most of the grated cheese until smooth (reserve just a little for the garnish). Return the soup to the pan, add the milk and salt and pepper to taste and stir to mix. Reheat until piping hot.

4. Meanwhile, toast the bread, sprinkle with the reserved cheese and grill or bake to melt.

5. To serve, ladle the soup into warmed bowls and top each with a piece of French toast. Sprinkle with chopped parsley or thyme and serve at once.

TIP

Other edible squashes can be used to make this soup. If using small round squash why not keep the scooped out shells and ladle the soup into them for serving? Takes care of the washing up too!

WILD ALASKA SALMON KORMA BAKE

This is a wonderful, lightly-spiced, curried, family main meal dish. It is equally good made with either cooked fresh salmon or canned salmon (so makes a good store cupboard standby). Make it in a large roasting tin for a one-pot meal or, to make this meal easier to serve, cook in individual baking dishes.

SERVES 4

400g cooked fresh wild Alaska salmon or 2 x 213g cans red or pink wild Alaska salmon

500g butternut squash, peeled and cut into chunks

2 tbsp olive oil

½ tsp cumin seeds

salt and freshly ground black pepper

1 small cauliflower, broken into florets

150g fine green beans, trimmed and halved

300g low-fat natural yogurt

2 tbsp Korma curry paste

2 tbsp mango chutney

2 tbsp chopped fresh coriander

4 poppadoms, lightly crushed

1. Preheat the oven if necessary to 170˚C/Fan 150˚C/Esse Dial Guide MODERATE. (Aim for the dial reading to be in the middle of MODERATE).

2. Skin the cooked fresh salmon and break into chunks or drain the canned salmon (discarding the liquid, skin and bones) and flake into large pieces.

3. Put the butternut squash in a large roasting tin, add the oil, cumin seeds and salt and pepper to taste, tossing to coat. Roast for 25-30 minutes until tender, turning once.

4. Meanwhile, cook the cauliflower in lightly salted boiling water for 3-4 minutes. Add the green beans and cook for a further 3-4 minutes. Drain well and add to the cooked squash with the chunks of salmon.

5. Mix the yogurt with the curry paste, mango chutney and coriander. Spoon over the vegetables and salmon, then sprinkle with the poppadoms. Bake for 10-15 minutes until piping hot. Serve at once.

TIP

Vary the hotness of this curried dish according to your preferred taste. This recipe uses mild strength Korma paste but experiment with medium Madras, Tikka Masala or Passanda strengths or spicy and hot Jalfrezi and Vindaloo.

FIVE SPICED PORK WITH ROOTS

Bring a touch of the Orient to a Sunday lunchtime in Autumn with this wonderfully spicy and slightly sweet flavoured roast. Pork offers great value for money and when served with root vegetables in season has a great taste. Vary the roots if liked to include parsnips, beetroot, salsify, celeriac and swede.

SERVES 6

2 tsp Chinese 5 spice powder

3 tbsp olive oil

15g fine sea salt

1.3kg pork loin roast, rind scored

2 tsp grated root ginger

1 tbsp toasted sesame oil

½ tsp chilli flakes (optional)

3 large floury potatoes, peeled and cut into chunks

6 carrots, scrubbed and trimmed

6 small turnips, scrubbed and trimmed

2 sticks celery, each cut into 3 pieces

fresh herbs, to garnish (optional)

1. Preheat the oven if necessary to 200°C/Fan 180°C/Esse Dial Guide HOT. (Aim for the dial reading to be in the middle of HOT).

2. Rub the Chinese 5 spice powder, 1 tbsp of the oil and the salt over the pork, making sure it gets into the cuts in the rind. Place on a rack over a roasting tin and cook for 1 hour.

3. Mix together the remaining oil with the ginger, sesame oil and chilli if used in a second roasting tin. Add the potatoes, carrots, turnips and celery, tossing well.

4. Pour the fat and juices from the pork over the vegetables and return both to the oven (place the vegetables above the pork). Roast for a further 1 hour, turning the vegetables once, until both are tender and cooked.

5. Allow the pork to rest in a warm place, wrapped in foil, before slicing to serve with the roasted vegetables. Garnish with a few fresh herbs if liked.

VARIATION

Summer 5 Spiced Pork:
Prepare as above but use a selection of Summer vegetables like sliced courgettes, quartered peppers, wedges of red onion, cubes of aubergine and whole cloves of garlic instead of the roots. Roast for the final 40 minutes of the cooking time.

SAFFRON POACHED PEARS WITH PARMIGIANO-REGGIANO

This poached pear dessert is so simple to make, yet it tastes utterly divine! The secret is that it's not too sweet and the Parmigiano-Reggiano and ricotta filling complements the pears perfectly.

SERVES 4

150g Parmigiano-Reggiano cheese

150g ricotta cheese

6 pears (not too ripe), peeled, halved and cored

600ml medium white wine

50g caster sugar

strip of lemon zest

generous pinch of saffron

2 star anise

1. Grate the Parmigiano-Reggiano very finely. Add the ricotta, mix well then cover and set aside until ready to serve.

2. Put the pears, wine and sugar in a large pan with the lemon zest, saffron and star anise. Heat and simmer very gently for about 20 minutes, until the pears are tender. Remove from the heat and cool until barely warm.

3. Divide the pears, with some of the flavoured syrup, between 4 serving bowls. Spoon the cheese mixture onto the pears and serve.

GET AHEAD!

The pears can be made up to 3 days in advance, then covered and chilled until required. Warm them slightly before serving to enjoy them at their best.

LEMON TART WITH FRESH FRUIT TOPPING

This creamy lemon tart is perfect all year round but especially good in the late Summer or Autumn months when fruit choice for the topping is abundant. The fruit selection in the photograph gives some ideas but feel free to choose your own favourites.

SERVES 8

1 recipe sweet pastry (page 86)

Filling:

3 eggs

160g caster sugar

grated zest and juice of 2 lemons

160g butter, melted

90g ground almonds

Topping:

selection of fresh fruit like sliced green apples (dipped in lemon juice), sliced fresh or canned peaches, apricots and pears, sliced strawberries, sliced kiwi, blackberries, blueberries, raspberries, sliced and halved grapes

mint sprigs, to decorate (optional)

1. Preheat the oven if necessary to 190°C/Fan 170°C/Esse Dial Guide HOT. (Aim for the dial reading to be at the low end of HOT).

2. Make the pastry according to the recipe instructions. Roll out and line a 23cm fluted flan tin and chill for 10 minutes. Cover with foil and weight with baking beans then bake 'blind' for 15 minutes. Remove the foil and beans and cook for a further 5 minutes.

3. Meanwhile, whisk the eggs and sugar until they are very thick. Stir in the lemon zest and juice then the melted butter and almonds. Pour into the prepared pastry case. Bake for 25-30 minutes, or until the filling is golden and set. Allow to cool.

4. To serve, top the tart with a selection of fresh fruit and decorate with mint sprigs if liked. Cut into wedges to serve with cream, crème fraîche, yogurt or ice cream.

GET AHEAD!

The tart can be made up to 24 hours ahead but to avoid the fruit drying out, glaze with a mixture of 2 tbsp apricot jam warmed until syrupy with 2 tbsp water. Spoon over the fruit when cooled but still liquid.

PENNE WITH ROAST SHALLOTS AND PUMPKIN SEEDS

This is a delicious vegetarian pasta dish with contrasting flavours and textures from the soft shallots and pumpkin, to the al dente pasta (with a bite) and the crunchy pumpkin seeds.

SERVES 4

1 small pumpkin

2 tbsp olive oil

salt and freshly ground black pepper

20 small shallots, peeled

300g dried penne pasta

1 chilli, seeded and finely sliced

15g butter

6 tbsp water

1 sprig rosemary, chopped

grated Parmesan cheese, to serve

1. Preheat the oven if necessary to 180°C/Fan 160°C/Esse Dial Guide MODERATE. (Aim for the dial reading to be at the top end of MODERATE or the very low end of HOT).

2. Peel and cut the pumpkin into bite-sized pieces, reserving the pumpkin seeds. Place the pumpkin in a pan with the olive oil and salt and pepper to taste. Sauté for about 5 minutes until coloured on the outside. Add the shallots and cook for a further 5-10 minutes. Remove from the pan and set aside.

3. Meanwhile, cook the pasta in boiling, salted water according to the packet instructions. Drain, rinse and keep warm. Toast the pumpkin seeds in the oven for 5 minutes.

4. Return a quarter of the pumpkin and shallot mixture to the pan with the chilli, butter, water and rosemary. Heat through to make a bubbly sauce. Add the remaining pumpkin mixture then finally fold in the cooked pasta.

5. Serve on warmed plates dusted with a little Parmesan cheese and scattered with the pumpkin seeds.

VARIATION

Those who miss meat might welcome the addition of some cooked and sliced spicy sausage at the end of cooking.

STICKY GINGER AND BEETROOT MUFFINS

These muffins have a dark side to them... from the beetroot added to give colour and flavour. Great for Hallowe'en, they provide a sweet, sticky end to the festivities!

MAKES 12 LARGE MUFFINS

200g golden syrup

200g black treacle

150g unsalted butter

125g dark brown sugar

100g stem ginger, finely chopped

4 tsp ground ginger

2 tsp ground cinnamon

250g pack cooked beetroot

250ml milk

2 medium eggs, beaten

1 tsp bicarbonate of soda

300g plain flour

Icing:

150g icing sugar

zest of 1 lemon, plus 1 tbsp lemon juice

1. Preheat the oven if necessary to 180°C/Fan 160°C/Esse Dial Guide MODERATE. (Aim for the dial reading to be at the top end of MODERATE or very low end of HOT). Line a large 12-hole muffin tray with cases.

2. Place the golden syrup, black treacle, butter, sugar, stem ginger, ground ginger and cinnamon in a pan and warm until the butter and sugar have melted.

3. Meanwhile, purée the beetroot with the milk, eggs and bicarbonate of soda. Add to the slightly cooled sugar mixture, mixing well.

4. Sift the flour into a bowl then beat in the beetroot mixture until the mixture is smooth.

5. Divide between the muffin cases. Bake for 15-20 minutes or until firm but springy to the touch. Be careful not to overcook the muffins, they are nice a little sticky. Remove from the tray and leave to cool on a rack.

6. While the muffins are cooling make the icing. Mix the icing sugar with the lemon zest and lemon juice to make a smooth paste. Drizzle over the muffins when completely cold.

GET AHEAD!

These muffins keep really well for up to 4 days if stored in an airtight tin.

ROASTED TOMATO SOUP WITH CRISPY BACON

This wonderfully warming soup is made with English vine-ripened tomatoes that are oven-roasted to bring out their natural sweetness. It's perfect to serve on Bonfire Night with crusty bread. For outdoor eating serve in warmed mugs.

SERVES 4

950g English vine-ripened tomatoes, quartered

2 red onions, finely sliced

4 cloves garlic, crushed

1 tbsp olive oil

salt and freshly ground black pepper

6 rashers dry cure smoked streaky bacon

1 litre hot vegetable stock

4 tsp balsamic vinegar

1. Preheat the oven if necessary to 220°C/Fan 200°C/Esse Dial Guide HOT. (Aim for the dial reading to be at the top end of HOT).

2. Place the tomatoes, red onion and garlic in a roasting tin. Drizzle with the olive oil and season with salt and freshly ground black pepper to taste. Roast for 20 minutes until softened and slightly charred.

3. Meanwhile, put the bacon on a rack set over a baking tray and place in the oven for the last 15 minutes of the tomatoes cooking time. Remove when crisp, leave until cool then break into pieces.

4. Bring the stock to the boil in a large pan, add the roasted tomato mixture and mix well. Purée until smooth.

5. Reheat if necessary then ladle into warmed bowls or mugs. Drizzle with the balsamic vinegar and scatter with the crispy bacon to serve.

VARIATION

This soup is also delicious served cold in the warm Summer months. Prepare as above, chill and serve drizzled with balsamic vinegar and torn Parma ham rather than crispy bacon.

MINI SAUSAGE WRAPS WITH CRISPY ONIONS

Wraps, filled with sticky sausages and onions, make great Bonfire Night fare. Children will love these as they are sweet and easy to eat. For a more adult party try other speciality and spicy sausages and perhaps add some tongue-tingling mustard or chilli relish to the wraps.

MAKES 6

12 pork chipolata sausages

2 red onions, cut into wedges

1 tbsp sunflower or vegetable oil

2 tbsp tomato ketchup

1 tbsp clear honey

1 tbsp dark brown muscovado sugar

1 tbsp ordinary dark or Indonesian sweet soy sauce

6 plain or seeded tortilla wraps

1. Preheat the oven if necessary to 220°C/Fan 200°C/Esse Dial Guide HOT. (Aim for the dial reading to be at the top end of HOT).

2. Line a roasting tin or baking tray with baking parchment or easy glide. Place the sausages and onion wedges on top.

3. In a small bowl, mix the oil with the tomato ketchup, honey, sugar and soy sauce. Drizzle over the sausages and onion wedges and toss to coat well. Bake for 20-25 minutes, until the sausages are thoroughly cooked and have browned without burning, and the onion wedges are starting to crisp.

4. To serve, place 2 of the sausages and some onion wedges on each wrap and fold up to enclose. Allow to cool a little then serve with napkins.

TIP

Vegetarians can still be catered for with this recipe, simply replace the traditional meat sausages with Quorn sausages or Quorn fajita style strips (cooked according to the pack instructions).

BONFIRE PUMPKIN PILAF WITH ALMONDS

The wonderfully fragrant smell of the onions and spices cooking at the beginning of this recipe will entice Bonfire Night revellers into the kitchen. It's a good basic recipe using quick or easy-cook basmati rice. For meat eaters I often add cooked chicken and chorizo and for vegetarians crumbled feta, grilled halloumi cheese or extra roasted vegetables.

SERVES 6

2 tbsp olive oil

2 tbsp butter

1 onion, chopped

3 cloves garlic, peeled and sliced

1 tbsp cumin seeds

1 tbsp fennel seeds

1 tsp black onion seeds

400g quick or easy-cook basmati rice

400g diced pumpkin

800ml hot vegetable stock

salt and freshly ground black pepper

125g thick Greek yogurt

100g radishes, sliced

100g roasted almonds, crushed

small bunch fresh mint and coriander, coarsely chopped

1 chilli, seeded and finely sliced

1. Heat the oil and butter in a large, heavy-based pan (with tight-fitting lid). Add the onion, garlic, cumin, fennel and black onions seeds and cook for 3 minutes.

2. Add the rice and cook for 2 minutes. Add the pumpkin and stock. Bring to the boil, reduce the heat to a simmer, add salt and pepper to taste, cover and cook, without stirring, for 10 minutes, or until all the stock has been absorbed. (If you're using regular rice then this may take up to 20-25 minutes cooking time). At this point add any meat or vegetarian extras, remove from the heat, re-cover and leave to stand for 5 minutes to finish cooking.

3. Remove the lid and give the pilaf a gentle stir. Top with the yogurt, scatter with the radishes and almonds then sprinkle with the mint, coriander and chilli to serve.

TIP

Younger members of the family may not appreciate the fiery taste or heat of the chillies added at the end of this recipe. Serve them first, then add the chillies for more mature tastes to keep everyone happy.

WINT❄R

Winter... with either crisp blue skies and frost on the ground or dismal grey clouds and incessant drizzle... signals the start of a very special series of seasonal celebrations – Christmas, New Year, Chinese New Year and Valentine's Day.

Either way, with shorter days and chilly weather it's good to stay indoors and prepare for these holiday feasts. Classic and family passed-down traditional favourite recipes will almost always win against new offerings but an unfamiliar and therefore welcome dish might just ring the changes. Here are a few.

CHRISTMAS & NEW YEAR

THE MAIN EVENT

Roast Turkey with Apricot and Couscous Stuffing, roast potatoes, seasonal vegetables and cranberry sauce *or*

Baked Gammon with a Quince and Sherry Glaze with new potatoes or colcannon and seasonal vegetables *or*

Roast Rump of Beef with Garlic and Thyme with roasted butternut squash wedges, Yorkshire pudding and seasonal vegetables *or*

Chestnut, Red Pepper and Red Leicester Strudel with seasonal vegetables or mixed salad

SWEET TREAT

Pink Lady Apple and Mince Pies

CHINESE NEW YEAR

Hot, Sour and Sweet Prawn Stir-Fry *or*

Singapore Vegetable Chow Mein

VALENTINE'S DAY

Tenderstem, Peach and Goat's Cheese Salad with crusty ciabatta

Pan Fried Salmon with Shallot Lyonnaise Potatoes

ROAST TURKEY WITH APRICOT AND COUSCOUS STUFFING

Everyone has their favourite turkey and stuffing recipe... sometimes handed down the family over generations. This is a new take on an old favourite, instead of the usual sausage meat and chestnut stuffing it has a modern and lighter couscous one.

SERVES 6 (WITH LEFTOVERS)

150g dried couscous

2 cloves garlic, crushed

1 small onion, finely chopped

150g courgette, coarsely grated

1 tbsp chopped fresh sage

50g soft dried apricots, finely chopped or dried cranberries

25g toasted flaked almonds

salt and freshly ground black pepper

5kg whole turkey

6 thin slices lean bacon, halved

2 oranges, cut into wedges

300ml dry white wine or turkey stock

bay leaves, to garnish (optional)

1. Preheat the oven to 190°C/Fan 170°C/Esse Dial Guide HOT. (Aim for the dial reading to be at the low end of HOT).

2. Put the couscous in a bowl and add sufficient boiling water to cover by 1cm. Leave to stand for 10 minutes then fluff with a fork. Add the garlic, onion, courgette, sage, apricots or cranberries, almonds and salt and pepper to taste. Spoon into small bun tins lined with the bacon.

3. Place the orange wedges inside the turkey and place in a roasting tin. Pour in the wine or stock and cover with foil. Roast for 3½ hours, removing the foil for the final 20-30 minutes to brown the skin. Allow to rest, covered with foil, for up to 1 hour before serving.

4. Cook the stuffing in the oven during this time for 20-30 minutes.

5. Make a gravy in the usual way with any skimmed pan juices. Serve the turkey garnished with bay leaves if liked and with the stuffing, gravy and chosen vegetables.

GET AHEAD!

The stuffing can be used to stuff the neck cavity of the turkey if preferred but must be cold before doing so. Check the turkey is cooked sufficiently by piercing the thickest part of the thigh with a skewer — the juices that run out should be clear with no traces of pink.

BAKED GAMMON WITH A QUINCE AND SHERRY GLAZE

A sweet, sticky glaze of quince paste and sherry perfectly complements the flavours of this traditional Christmas gammon. It's delicious both hot and cold.

SERVES 8

2.5kg smoked gammon joint

1 litre pressed apple juice

30-35 whole cloves

100ml fino sherry

155g pot quince paste
(I used Cano's Membrillo pure Spanish quince paste)

1. Preheat the oven if necessary to 180°C/Fan 160°C/Esse Dial Guide MODERATE. (Aim for the dial reading to be at the top end of MODERATE or very low end of HOT).

2. Place the gammon in a large pan. Add the apple juice and enough cold water to cover. Bring to the boil, cover then simmer for 1 hour.

3. Drain the gammon and allow to cool slightly. Remove any string, then, with a sharp knife, carefully cut away the rind, leaving the layer of fat intact. Score the fat with a diamond pattern and stud the centre of each with a clove. Place on a rack in a roasting tin, cover with foil and roast for 45 minutes.

4. Meanwhile, place the sherry and quince paste in a small pan and gentle heat until melted. Simmer for 2-3 minutes. Spoon about half of the glaze over the gammon. Pour a little water into the base of the roasting tin to prevent the juices from burning, re-cover then roast for another 20-25 minutes.

5. Uncover the gammon, brush with more glaze and roast, uncovered, until golden. Allow to stand for 10 minutes before carving to serve hot.

TIP

Any remaining glaze can be brushed over chicken breasts or pork chops before grilling or baking.

ROAST RUMP OF BEEF WITH GARLIC AND THYME

Christmas and holiday eating doesn't just have to be about turkey and ham. This might be the time to splash out on a special British beef top rump roast. In this recipe the beef is marinated before cooking with garlic and thyme then roasted with slices of butternut squash.

SERVES 4-6

4 cloves garlic, chopped

2 tbsp fresh thyme leaves

2 shallots, peeled and sliced

3 tbsp olive oil

salt and freshly ground black pepper

850g British beef top rump roast

700g sliced butternut squash

1. Mix the garlic, thyme, shallots, olive oil and seasoning to taste in a dish. Add the beef, cover and chill for 1½-2 hours or overnight, turning twice.

2. Preheat the oven if necessary to 200°C/Fan 180°C/Esse Dial Guide HOT. (Aim for the dial reading to be in the middle of HOT).

3. Remove the beef from the marinade. Add the squash to the leftover marinade and toss to coat. Heat a roasting tin on the hob over a high heat and brown the beef quickly on all sides. Transfer to the oven and roast according to how you like your beef cooked (see ROASTING GUIDELINE opposite). Cook for the calculated time, adding the squash for the last 30 minutes. (This may mean that the squash is cooked from the beginning for a rare piece of beef).

4. Cover with foil and rest for 10 minutes before carving.

ROASTING GUIDELINE

Allow 20 minutes per 500g for rare beef; 25 minutes per 500g for medium beef; and 30 minutes per 500g for well done beef.

CHESTNUT, RED PEPPER AND RED LEICESTER STRUDEL

Here is something a little more festive than the traditional nut roast for those who are vegetarian or those who choose to forgo meat over the holiday celebrations. Serve warm with seasonal vegetables or cold with a crisp mixed salad.

SERVES 4

1 tbsp olive oil

1 onion, chopped

1 clove garlic, crushed

200g chestnut mushrooms, wiped and roughly chopped

100g canned peeled chestnuts

salt and freshly ground black pepper

4 sheets filo pastry

15g butter, melted

150g Red Leicester cheese, grated

300g jar red pimientos, drained and trimmed

1 tsp sesame seeds

1. Preheat the oven if necessary to 200°C/Fan 180°C/Esse Dial Guide HOT. (Aim for the dial reading to be in the middle of HOT).

2. Heat the oil in a pan, add the onion, garlic and mushrooms, mixing well. Cover and cook gently for 5 minutes. Uncover, increase the heat and cook until the juices from the mushrooms have evaporated.

3. Transfer to a food processor, add the chestnuts and seasoning to taste and blend until you have a chunky pâté type consistency.

4. Lay a sheet of filo pastry on a clean surface, brush with a little melted butter. Top with another sheet and repeat until you have a stack of 4 sheets. Spread the chestnut mixture over the top to within 2.5cm of the edge. Top with the cheese and red pimiento. Starting from one end, roll up like a Swiss roll to enclose the filling and place on a baking tray. Brush with any remaining butter and sprinkle with the sesame seeds.

5. Bake for 20-25 minutes or until the pastry is crisp and golden. Serve warm cut into slices.

GET AHEAD!

The strudel can be prepared up to 24 hours ahead of cooking. Cover and chill in the refrigerator until required. Uncover and bake from chilled for 25-30 minutes until crisp and golden.

PINK LADY APPLE AND MINCE PIES

Shop-bought mince pies rarely taste better than home-made and these with their apple and dried cranberry filling are more than impressive. Serve warm or cold with cream or custard if liked.

MAKES 12

Pastry:

50g cold butter, diced

50g lard or solid vegetable oil, diced

175g plain flour

2 tbsp icing sugar

1 egg yolk

4 tbsp cold water

Filling:

200g mincemeat

1 Pink Lady apple, cored and finely chopped

25g dried cranberries

icing sugar, to dust

1. Preheat the oven if necessary to 200°C/Fan 180°C/Esse Dial Guide HOT. (Aim for the dial reading to be in the middle of HOT).

2. Put the butter and lard (or solid vegetable oil) into a food processor along with the flour, icing sugar, egg yolk and water and pulse until the mixture binds together. Alternatively, use your fingertips to rub the butter and lard lightly through the flour and icing sugar, until the mixture resembles breadcrumbs, then add the egg yolk and sufficient water to bind together. Turn the pastry onto a lightly floured surface, knead to a ball then roll out and stamp out 12 circles with a 7cm cutter. Line a bun tin with these and chill for 30 minutes. Reserve the pastry trimmings.

3. Meanwhile, mix the mincemeat with the apple and cranberries and spoon into the pastry cases. Stamp out 12 stars from the pastry trimmings and place one on the top of each pastry case.

4. Bake for 15-20 minutes until lightly golden and cooked. Serve warm or cold dusted with icing sugar.

GET AHEAD!

Baked mince pies will keep in the refrigerator in an airtight container for up to 3 days. Ideally warm in the oven for 5-8 minutes before serving.

HOT, SOUR AND SWEET PRAWN STIR-FRY

Fiery from the chilli; sour from the tangy tamarind; and naturally sweet from the delicious Pink Lady apples... this is a Chinese New Year dish to tickle the taste buds. Try and choose a stir-fry vegetable mix that has lots of different colours and flavours, or make up your own selection. Serve with steamed rice instead of noodles if you prefer.

SERVES 4

100g dried egg noodles

100g Tenderstem broccoli

2 tbsp groundnut oil

1 Pink Lady apple, cored and sliced into strips

200g raw peeled king prawns

3 tsp tamarind paste

1 red chilli, finely sliced

260g pack fresh stir-fry vegetables (or your own mix)

2 tbsp soy sauce

1 tbsp sesame oil

½ tsp Thai fish sauce

1. Cook the noodles according to the packet instructions, drain, rinse and keep warm. Meanwhile, cut the florets off the broccoli and finely slice the stems and set aside.

2. Heat half of the groundnut oil in a wok or large frying pan. Add the apple slices and stir-fry for 3 minutes or until lightly browned. Transfer to a plate. Add the prawns and 2 tsp of the tamarind paste and cook for 2-3 minutes until almost cooked. Remove the prawns and keep with the apples.

3. Add the remaining groundnut oil to the pan and stir-fry the chilli, stir-fry vegetables and broccoli for 4 minutes.

4. Finally, return the prawns and apples to the pan and stir in the soy sauce, sesame oil, fish sauce and remaining tamarind. Cook for 1-2 minutes then serve with the noodles.

TIP

Make up your own stir-fry mixture by combining ingredients like sliced dwarf corn, chopped spring onions, strips of red and yellow pepper, discs of crunchy water chestnuts or julienne of bamboo shoots for a colourful vegetable medley.

SINGAPORE VEGETABLE CHOW MEIN

This is a tasty noodle dish where the vegetables are flavoured with ginger, garlic and a touch of curry powder. A good vegetarian option it can also suit meat eaters if two finely sliced or shredded duck breasts are added to the mixture at the last stage of cooking with the noodles.

SERVES 4

250g egg noodles

1 tbsp toasted sesame oil

1 red pepper, cored, seeded and sliced

100g shitake mushrooms, wiped and sliced

75g mangetout

75g spring onions, sliced

100g bean sprouts

½ tsp garlic granules

1 tbsp medium curry powder

½ tsp ground ginger

½ tsp crushed chillies

1½ tsp light soy sauce

5 tsp Shaoxing rice wine (or dry sherry)

1. Prepare the noodles according to the packet instructions, drain and rinse.

2. Heat the oil in a wok or large deep frying pan. Add the pepper, mushrooms, mangetout, spring onions and beansprouts and stir-fry for 4-5 minutes.

3. Add the garlic granules, curry powder, ginger, chillies, soy sauce, rice wine and cooked noodles. Continue to stir-fry for a further 2 minutes then serve at once.

TIP

Toasted sesame oil gives a good authentic flavour to this stir-fried dish but chilli or wok oil (where the oil is infused with garlic and ginger) can also be used.

TENDERSTEM, PEACH AND GOAT'S CHEESE SALAD

This simple but stylish salad starter is bursting with freshness and flavour and just the thing to start a Valentine's Day meal. I think it is delicious with a little crusty ciabatta bread to soak up the juices.

SERVES 2

100g Tenderstem broccoli, stems cut in half

2 medium peaches, stoned and quartered

1½ tsp olive oil

salt and freshly ground black pepper

50g baby spinach leaves

75g goat's cheese log (I used Kidderton Ash), cut into thin slices

few fresh basil leaves, torn into pieces

Dressing:

2 tbsp extra virgin olive oil

1 tbsp balsamic vinegar

1. Preheat a griddle pan until smoking hot... this may take up to 10 minutes.

2. In a medium bowl, toss the Tenderstem broccoli and peach quarters in the olive oil with salt and pepper to taste.

3. Add the peach and broccoli mixture to the griddle and cook for about 5 minutes, turning a few times, until they are just tender and marked with griddle-lines.

4. Arrange the spinach leaves on a serving plate and top with the cooked peach and broccoli mixture. Add the goat's cheese and sprinkle with the basil leaves.

5. Beat the extra virgin olive oil with the balsamic vinegar and salt and pepper to taste to make a dressing. Drizzle over the salad and serve at once.

TIP

When available replace the peaches in this salad with 2 fresh, ripe nectarines or 4-6 fresh, ripe apricots... they are equally as delicious.

PAN FRIED SALMON WITH SHALLOT LYONNAISE POTATOES

There's nothing much more enticing than a crispy skin salmon fillet on a bed of shallot sautéed potatoes with a herby tomato dressing... unless it's second helpings! This recipe also works well with other fish fillets like sea bass, but equally as good with a meat fillet of your choice.

SERVES 2

200g new potatoes

50ml vegetable oil

4 large shallots, peeled and finely chopped

100ml white wine

5g fresh basil, coarsely chopped

2g fresh tarragon, coarsely chopped

10g snipped chives

10g fresh flat-leaf parsley, coarsely chopped

juice of ½ lemon

1 large tomato, skinned, seeded and chopped

salt and freshly ground black pepper

15g butter

2 x 150g salmon fillets

1. Cook the potatoes in boiling salted water until tender, about 15 minutes. Drain, cut each potato in half and set aside.

2. Heat one-third of the oil in a pan, add half of the shallots and cook for 5 minutes. Add the white wine and cook until it has almost completely evaporated. Remove from the heat, add another one-third of the oil, the basil, tarragon, chives, parsley, lemon juice, tomato and salt and pepper to taste.

3. Heat most of the remaining oil in a large non-stick frying pan. Add the potatoes and cook until starting to colour. Add the remaining shallots, butter and seasoning to taste. Cook until golden.

4. Meanwhile, brush the salmon fillets with any remaining oil and cook in a non-stick pan until tender. Cook skin-side down first for about 4 minutes, until the skin is crispy, then turn over and cook for a further 1 minute.

5. To serve, spoon the potatoes onto a plate, spoon over the herby sauce and top with a salmon fillet.

TIP

If you're looking for a quick and easy dessert for Valentine's Day then nothing could be more indulgent than chocolate dipped strawberries. Dip whole, unhulled strawberries in melted chocolate (holding the stalk to assist with this), place on non-stick parchment and chill to set. Share of course!

INDEX

ACKNOWLEDGEMENTS

Recipe and Image Credits

As with all books, there are more people involved in the conception and production of the publication than the author's name on the jacket. I am personally indebted to all colleagues at Esse, Gill Meller (Head Chef at River Cottage), designer Andrea Rumsey and photographer Jemma Harding (pages 11, 33, 55 and 77) for their enthusiasm and support.

Countless food companies, growers, supermarkets and public relation agencies also helped with sourcing images and information for the recipes – their help has proved invaluable and I give thanks to them here.

Alaska Seafood Marketing Institute www.alaskaseafood.org (pages 29, 59)

Britegg
www.britegg.co.uk (page 53)

British Asparagus
www.british-asparagus.co.uk (pages 3, 10, 15)

British Carrots
www.britishcarrots.co.uk (page 49)

British Cheese
www.britishcheese.com (page 85)

British Onions
www.britishonions.co.uk (page 23)

Carol Bowen Ball
www.bariatriccookery.com (pages 6, 7, 19, 22)

Fenland Celery
www.lovecelery.co.uk (page 51)

I Love British Turkey
www.britishturkey.co.uk (page 43)

Jersey Royals
www.jerseyroyals.co.uk (page 13)

Love Beetroot
www.lovebeetroot.co.uk (pages 27, 69)

Love Radish
www.loveradish.co.uk (page 75)

Parma Ham Consortium
www.proscuittodiparma.com (page 25)

Parmigiano-Reggiano Cheese
www.parmigianoreggiano.com (pages 57, 63)

Pink Lady Apples
www.pinkladyapples.co.uk (pages 30, 31, 87, 89)

Schwartz
www.schwartz.co.uk (page 91)

Simply Beef and Lamb
www.simplybeefandlamb.co.uk (page 17)

Sweet Eve Strawberries
www.sweetevestrawberry.co.uk (pages 32, 46, 47)

Tenderstem Broccoli
www.tenderstem.co.uk (page 93)

UK Shallots
www.ukshallot.com (pages 40, 41, 54, 67, 95)

Viva Strawberries
www.vivastrawberries.com (page 37)

Waitrose, where more than 6,000 recipes can be viewed at www.waitrose.com (pages 3, 9, 12, 14, 21, 28, 35, 39, 42, 45, 52, 62, 66, 70, 71, 73, 74, 76, 79, 81, 83)

Links
www.esse.com